THE

SEVEN GREAT HYMNS

OF THE

Mediaeval Church.

Thou haſt no ſhore, fair Ocean!
Thou haſt no time, bright Day!
Dear Fountain of refreſhment
To pilgrims far away!

THIRD EDITION.

NEW YORK:
ANSON D. F. RANDOLPH,
770 BROADWAY, COR. OF 9TH ST.
1867.

CONTENTS.

	PAGE
The Celestial Country	1
Dies Iræ	44
Stabat Mater	96
Veni Sancte Spiritus	106
Veni Creator Spiritus	114
Vexilla Regis	120
The Alleluiatic Sequence	126
Appendix	134

TO THE READER.

THIS work was ſuggeſted by the intereſt felt in Mr. Prime's little book, the hymn, "*O Mother Dear Jeruſalem.*" It is publiſhed with a wiſh that it ſhall be placed beſide his, and that, finding the ſame welcome, it may yield, or perhaps revive, the ſame pleaſure and receive the ſame approval.

To ſave from years belonging to the darkened paſt thoughts of real, undeparted worth—to clothe theſe utterances in a dreſs neither too common for the requirements of our taſte, nor too good for our daily uſe—to do this in the hope that purer eyes will often reſt upon its pages, and a holy faith find refreſhment in its imagery—that ſome one better than its author will keep it always near, a ſecret, ſympathetic friend for lonely hours, or gather, in ſorrow, from its ſentences the conſolation which they poſſeſs—confeſſes the object for which it has exiſted, and to which it is devoted.

Theſe hopes, which were expreſſed in the firſt edition of this work, were fulfilled almoſt at the inſtant of its publication. And the aſſurances that its real object was attained were more grateful than even hope had promiſed. A continuing demand by the public has led to this reviſed edition, wherein ſome trivial errors are corrected, and two verſions of the *Dies Iræ* are added. The ſeven tranſlations now given will render, it is believed, the Engliſh expoſition of the Great Hymn complete.

New York, June, 1866.

THE

CELESTIAL COUNTRY.

BERNARD DE MORLAS, monk of Cluni, is not to be confounded with the great Bernard his contemporary, Abbot of Clairvaux, and Saint in the Romiſh calendar. The place of his nativity is uncertain, and the years of his birth and of his death are alike unknown. He lived during the firſt half of the twelfth century; he was born, according to one authority, at *Morlaix*, in Bretagne; according to another, at *Morlas*, in the lower Pyrenees; whilſt a third gives his birth-place to England, and claſſes him with her illuſtrious writers (*De illuſtribus Angliæ Scriptoribus*).[1] After ſeven centuries of comparative forgetfulneſs, the genius of two Engliſh ſcholars has revived a portion of his works; and hereafter his name will be beſt known in that country, which may poſſibly poſſeſs his birth-place.

There still survive of his writings five poems, the greatest of which is *De Contemptu Mundi.* It was written about 1145, and contains three thousand lines, divided into three books. In substance the poem is a satire, unforgiving and severe: in form it is in dactylic hexameter verse, wherein each line consists of three parts, and two of these parts rhyme with each other, while the lines themselves are in couplets of double rhyme. It is a verse pedantically called "leonine "and tailed rhyme, with lines in three parts, "between which a cæsura is not admissible."[2]

The poem commences thus:

Hora novis*sima,* || tempora pes*sima* || sunt, vigil*emus.*
Ecce min*aciter* || imminet arb*iter* || ille supr*emus.*
Imminet, imm*inet* || et mala term*inet,* || æqua co*ronet,*
Recta remun*eret,* || anxia lib*eret,* || æthera *donet,*
Auferat a*spera* || duraque pon*dera* || mentes *onustæ,*
Sobria mu*niat,* || improba pu*niat,* || utraque *juste.*

Hours of the latest! times of the basest! our vigil before us!
Judgment eternal of Being supernal now hanging o'er us!
Evil to terminate, equity vindicate, cometh the Kingly;
Righteousness seeing, anxious hearts freeing, crowning each singly,
Bearing life's weariness, tasting life's bitterness, life as it must be;
Th' righteous retaining, sinners arraigning, judging all justly.

This verſe, ſo difficult that the Engliſh language is incapable of expreſſing it, is continued through the three thouſand lines of the poem. In his preface the monk avows the belief that nothing but the ſpecial inſpiration of the SPIRIT of GOD enabled him to employ it through ſo long a poem. After recounting its difficulties, and alluding to the faint attempts of the two great verſifiers of his day, Hildebert de Lavardin and Wichard of Lyons, he exclaims: "I "may then aſſert, not in oſtentation, but with "humble confidence, that if I had not received "directly from on high the gift of inſpiration "and intelligence, I had not dared to attempt "an enterpriſe ſo little accorded to the powers "of the human mind."

"This work," ſays the author of the *Hiſtoire Littéraire de la France*, "was drawn from the duſt in 1483, and its publication "was achieved on the tenth of December of the ſame year, at "Paris, *in magni domo campi Gaillardi.* The Proteſtants, eager "to gather every thing which appears unfavorable to the Church "of Rome, have ſince multiplied the editions. Some Catholics "have alſo given to it ſome praiſes; and ſurely it merits them, "at leaſt by the ſentiments of piety which it exhales, and by the "zeal with which the author attacks the abuſes of his time."

"In holy Rome the only power is gold;
There all is bought—there every thing is ſold.
Becauſe ſhe is the very way to right,
There truth is periſhed by unholy ſleight.
Even as the wheel turns, Rome to evil turns,
Rome, that ſpreads fragrance as when incenſe burns.
Rome wrongs mankind, and teaches men the road
To flee far off from Righteouſneſs' abode!
To ſeek for ruinous and diſgraceful gain,
The pallium's ſelf with ſimony to ſtain.
If aught you wiſh, be ſure a goodly bribe
Will haſte the ſealing of the lingering ſcribe.
Riſe! follow! let your penny go before,
Seek boldly then the threſhold; fear no more
That any ſtumbling-blocks will bar the way,
The Pope's own favor you can get for pay—
Without that help, 'tis beſt to keep away."

The opening of this monkiſh ſatire on the corruptions of its barbarous age, glows with a deſcription of the Heavenly Land more beautiful than ever before was wrought in verſe. This a great ſcholar of our time has taken from the poem and brought within the reach and notice of the world (*Trench*). It alſo has been re-woven into ſimple Engliſh verſe, and has received the appropriate name of THE CELESTIAL COUNTRY.

The tranſlator of The Celestial Country is Dr. John Maſon Neale, Warden of Sackville College, Suſſex, England, the moſt ſucceſſful tranſlator of mediæval hymns, and one of the moſt varied and voluminous writers of the time. "Lays and Legends of the Church of England;" "A Church Hiſtory for Children;" ſeven volumes of romances; a hiſtory of Greece; a hiſtory of Portugal; of the Patriarchate of Alexandria, and of the Janſeniſt Church of Holland; a large number of tales and hymns for children, and a moſt learned and elaborate commentary on the Book of Pſalms, are included in the long catalogue of his works.

This ſcholar of Cambridge, and this monk of Cluni, have given to the religious world the ſweeteſt and deareſt religious poem that our language contains. Dr. Neale ſays that he looks upon the lines of Bernard "as the moſt *lovely*, "in the ſame way that the *Dies Iræ* is the moſt "ſublime, and the *Stabat Mater* the moſt pathetic "of mediæval poems," but his own poem may claim more juſtly that word. The Celestial Country is better than *De Contemptu Mundi.*

The beautiful ſimplicity of its artleſs, childlike lines portrays more naturally the fervid imagery of the monk. After ſeven hundred years of darkneſs, the holy fervor of Bernard re-kindles in it as warmly as when in the warmth of his devotion he believed himſelf ſpecially inſpired by the Moſt High. In another language, at another time, and among thoſe who can but dimly trace his name in the crumbling record of his works, the Rhyme of the poor monk re-lives to gladden the hearts of other Chriſtians, loved by ſuch as poſſeſs its faith, and treaſured by the gentleſt and the beſt of earth.[3]

THE
CELESTIAL COUNTRY.

DR. NEALE.

I.

THE world is very evil,
　The times are waxing late;
Be ſober and keep vigil,
　The Judge is at the gate—
The Judge that comes in mercy,
　The Judge that comes with might,
To terminate the evil,
　To diadem the right.
When the juſt and gentle Monarch
　Shall ſummon from the tomb,
Let man, the guilty, tremble,
　For Man, the God, ſhall doom!

2.

Arise, arise, good Christian,
Let right to wrong succeed;
Let penitential sorrow
To heavenly gladness lead—
To the light that hath no evening,
That knows nor moon nor sun,
The light so new and golden,
The light that is but one.

3.

And when the Sole-Begotten
Shall render up once more
The kingdom to the FATHER,
Whose own it was before,
Then glory yet unheard of
Shall shed abroad its ray,
Resolving all enigmas,
An endless Sabbath-day.

4.

Then, then from his oppressors
The Hebrew shall go free,

And celebrate in triumph
  The year of Jubilee;
And the sunlit Land that recks not
  Of tempest nor of fight,
Shall fold within its bosom
  Each happy Israelite—
The Home of fadeless splendor,
  Of flowers that fear no thorn,
Where they shall dwell as children,
  Who here as exiles mourn.

5.

Midst power that knows no limit,
  And wisdom free from bound,
The Beatific Vision
  Shall glad the Saints around—
The peace of all the faithful,
  The calm of all the blest,
Inviolate, unvaried,
  Divinest, sweetest, best.
Yes, peace! for war is needless—
  Yes, calm! for storm is past—
And goal from finished labor,
  And anchorage at last.

6.

That peace—but who may claim it?
  The guileless in their way,
Who keep the ranks of battle,
  Who mean the thing they say—
The peace that is for heaven,
  And shall be for the earth;
The palace that re-echoes
  With festal song and mirth;
The garden, breathing spices,
  The paradise on high;
Grace beautified to glory,
  Unceasing minstrelsy.

7.

There nothing can be feeble,
  There none can ever mourn,
There nothing is divided,
  There nothing can be torn.
'Tis fury, ill, and scandal,
  'Tis peaceless peace below;
Peace, endless, strifeless, ageless,
  The halls of Syon know.

8.

O happy, holy portion,
  Refection for the blest,
True vision of true beauty,
  Sweet cure of all distrest!
Strive, man, to win that glory;
  Toil, man, to gain that light;
Send hope before to grasp it,
  Till hope be lost in sight;
Till JESUS gives the portion
  Those blessed souls to fill—
The insatiate, yet satisfied,
  The full, yet craving still.

9.

That fulness and that craving
  Alike are free from pain,
Where thou, midst heavenly citizens,
  A home like theirs shalt gain.
Here is the warlike trumpet;
  There, life set free from sin,
When to the last Great Supper
  The faithful shall come in;

When the heavenly net is laden
  With fishes many and great
(So glorious in its fulness,
  Yet so inviolate);
And perfect from unperfected,
  And fall'n from those that stand,[4]
And the sheep-flock from the goat-herd
  Shall part on either hand.

10.

And these shall pass to torment,
  And those shall triumph then—
The new peculiar nation,
  Blest number of blest men.
Jerusalem demands them;
  They paid the price on earth,
And now shall reap the harvest
  In blissfulness and mirth—
The glorious holy people,
  Who evermore relied
Upon their Chief and Father,
  The King, the Crucified—
The sacred ransomed number
  Now bright with endless sheen,

Who made the Crofs their watchword
  Of Jesus Nazarene,
Who (fed with heavenly nectar
  Where foul-like odors play)
Draw out the endlefs leifure
  Of that long vernal day.

11.

And, through the facred lilies
  And flowers on every fide,
The happy dear-bought people
  Go wandering far and wide;
Their breafts are filled with gladnefs,
  Their mouths are tun'd to praife,
What time, now fafe for ever,
  On former fins they gaze:
The fouler was the error,
  The fadder was the fall,
The ampler are the praifes
  Of Him who pardoned all.

12.

Their one and only anthem,
  The fulnefs of His love,

Who gives inſtead of torment,
  Eternal joys above—
Inſtead of torment, glory;
  Inſtead of death, that life
Wherewith your happy Country,
  True Iſraelites, is rife.

13.

Brief life is here our portion,
  Brief ſorrow, ſhort-liv'd care;
The life that knows no ending—
  The tearleſs life, is there.

14.

O happy retribution!
  Short toil, eternal reſt;
For mortals and for ſinners
  A manſion with the bleſt!
That we ſhould look, poor wand'rers,
  To have our home on high!
That worms ſhould ſeek for dwelling,
  Beyond the ſtarry ſky!
To all one happy guerdon
  Of one celeſtial grace;

For all, for all, who mourn their fall,
  Is one eternal place.

15.

And martyrdom hath roses
  Upon that heavenly ground;
And white and virgin lilies
  For virgin-souls abound.
There grief is turned to pleasure—
  Such pleasure as below
No human voice can utter,
  No human heart can know;
And after fleshly scandal,
  And after this world's night,
And after storm and whirlwind,
  Is calm, and joy, and light.

16.

And now we fight the battle,
  But then shall wear the crown
Of full and everlasting
  And passionless renown:
And now we watch and struggle,

And now we live in hope,
And Syon, in her anguiſh,
With Babylon muſt cope;
But He whom now we truſt in
Shall then be ſeen and known,
And they that know and ſee Him
Shall have Him for their own.

17.

The miſerable pleaſures
Of the body ſhall decay;
The bland and flattering ſtruggles
Of the fleſh ſhall paſs away;
And none ſhall there be jealous,
And none ſhall there contend;
Fraud, clamor, guile—what ſay I?
All ill, all ill ſhall end!

18.

And there is David's Fountain,
And life in fulleſt glow;
And there the light is golden,
And milk and honey flow—

The light that hath no evening,
  The health that hath no sore,
The life that hath no ending,
  But lasteth evermore.

19.

There Jesus shall embrace us,
  There Jesus be embraced—
That spirit's food and sunshine
  Whence earthly love is chased.
Amidst the happy chorus,
  A place, however low,
Shall shew Him us, and shewing,
  Shall satiate evermo.

20.

By hope we struggle onward:
  While here we must be fed
By milk, as tender infants,
  But there by Living Bread.
The night was full of terror,
  The morn is bright with gladness;
The Cross becomes our harbor,
  And we triumph after sadness.

21.

And Jesus to His true ones
  Brings trophies fair to ſee ;
And Jesus ſhall be loved, and
  Beheld in Galilee—
Beheld, when morn ſhall waken,
  And ſhadows ſhall decay,
And each true-hearted ſervant
  Shall ſhine as doth the day ;
And every ear ſhall hear it—
  "*Behold thy King's array,*
Behold thy God *in beauty,*
  The Law hath paſs'd away!"

22.

Yes! God my King and Portion,
  In fulneſs of Thy grace,
We then ſhall ſee for ever,
  And worſhip face to face.
Then Jacob into Iſrael,
  From earthlier ſelf eſtranged,
And Leah into Rachel
  For ever ſhall be changed;[5]

Then all the halls of Syon
   For aye ſhall be complete,
And in the Land of Beauty,
   All things of beauty meet.

23.

For thee, O dear, dear Country!
   Mine eyes their vigils keep;
For very love, beholding
   Thy happy name, they weep.
The mention of thy glory
   Is unction to the breaſt,
And medicine in ſickneſs,
   And love, and life, and reſt.

24.

O one, O onely Manſion!
   O Paradiſe of Joy!
Where tears are ever baniſhed,
   And ſmiles have no alloy,
Beſide thy living waters
   All plants are, great and ſmall,
The cedar of the foreſt,

The hyſſop of the wall ;
With jaſpers glow thy bulwarks,
Thy ſtreets with emeralds blaze,
The ſardius and the topaz
Unite in thee their rays ;
Thine ageleſs walls are bonded
With amethyſt unpriced ;
Thy Saints build up its fabric,
And the corner-ſtone is CHRIST.[6]

25.

The Croſs is all thy ſplendor,
The Crucified thy praiſe ;
His laud and benediction
Thy ranſomed people raiſe :
" JESUS, *the Gem of Beauty,*
True GOD *and Man*," they ſing,
" *The never-failing Garden,*
The ever-golden Ring ;
The Door, the Pledge, the Huſband,
The Guardian of his Court ;
The Day-ſtar of Salvation,
The Porter and the Port !"

26.

THOU HAST NO SHORE, FAIR OCEAN!
  THOU HAST NO TIME, BRIGHT DAY!
DEAR FOUNTAIN OF REFRESHMENT
  TO PILGRIMS FAR AWAY!
UPON THE ROCK OF AGES
  THEY RAISE THY HOLY TOWER;
THINE IS THE VICTOR'S LAUREL,
  AND THINE THE GOLDEN DOWER!

27.

Thou feel'ſt in myſtic rapture,
  O Bride that know'ſt no guile,
The Prince's ſweeteſt kiſſes,
  The Prince's lovelieſt ſmile;
Unfading lilies, bracelets
  Of living pearl thine own;
The LAMB is ever near thee,
  The Bridegroom thine alone.
The Crown is He to guerdon,
  The Buckler to protect,
And He Himſelf the Manſion,
  And He the Architect.

28.

The only art thou needest—
  Thanksgiving for thy lot;
The only joy thou seekest—
  The Life where Death is not.
And all thine endless leisure,
  In sweetest accents, sings
The ill that was thy merit,
  The wealth that is thy King's!

29.

JERUSALEM THE GOLDEN,
  WITH MILK AND HONEY BLEST,
BENEATH THY CONTEMPLATION
  SINK HEART AND VOICE OPPRESSED.
I KNOW NOT, O I KNOW NOT,
  WHAT SOCIAL JOYS ARE THERE!
WHAT RADIANCY OF GLORY,
  WHAT LIGHT BEYOND COMPARE!

30.

And when I fain would sing them,
  My spirit fails and faints;

And vainly would it image
  The assembly of the Saints.

31.

They stand, those halls of Syon,
  Conjubilant with song,
And bright with many an angel,
  And all the martyr throng;
The Prince is ever in them,
  The daylight is serene;
The pastures of the Blessed
  Are decked in glorious sheen.

32.

There is the Throne of David,
  And there, from care released,
The song of them that triumph,
  The shout of them that feast;
And they who, with their Leader,
  Have conquered in the fight,
For ever and for ever
  Are clad in robes of white![7]

33.

O holy, placid harp-notes
Of that eternal hymn!
O sacred, sweet refection,
And peace of Seraphim!
O thirst, for ever ardent,
Yet evermore content!
O true peculiar vision
Of God cunctipotent!
Ye know the many mansions
For many a glorious name,
And divers retributions
That divers merits claim;
For midst the constellations
That deck our earthly sky,
This star than that is brighter—
And so it is on high.

34.

Jerusalem the glorious!
The glory of the Elect!
O dear and future vision
That eager hearts expect!

Even now by faith I see thee,
  Even here thy walls discern;
To thee my thoughts are kindled,
  And strive, and pant, and yearn.

35.

Jerusalem the onely,
  That look'st from heaven below,
In thee is all my glory,
  In me is all my woe;
And though my body may not,
  My spirit seeks thee fain,
Till flesh and earth return me
  To earth and flesh again.

36.

O none can tell thy bulwarks,
  How gloriously they rise!
O none can tell thy capitals
  Of beautiful device!
Thy loveliness oppresses
  All human thought and heart:
And none, O peace, O Syon,
  Can sing thee as thou art!

37.

New mansion of new people,
Whom God's own love and light
Promote, increase, make holy,
Identify, unite!
Thou City of the Angels!
Thou City of the Lord!
Whose everlasting music
Is the glorious decachord![8]

38.

And there the band of Prophets
United praise ascribes,
And there the twelvefold chorus
Of Israel's ransomed tribes,
The lily-beds of virgins,
The roses' martyr-glow,
The cohort of the Fathers
Who kept the Faith below.

39.

And there the Sole-Begotten
Is Lord in regal state—

He, Judah's myſtic Lion,
  He, Lamb Immaculate.
O fields that know no ſorrow!
  O ſtate that fears no ſtrife!
O princely bowers! O land of flowers!
  O realm and home of Life!

40.

Jeruſalem, exulting
  On that ſecureſt ſhore,
I hope thee, wiſh thee, ſing thee,
  And love thee evermore!
I aſk not for my merit,
  I ſeek not to deny
My merit is deſtruction,
  A child of wrath am I;
But yet with Faith I venture
  And Hope upon my way;
For thoſe perennial guerdons
  I labor night and day.

41.

The beſt and deareſt FATHER,
  Who made me and who ſaved,

Bore with me in defilement,
  And from defilement laved,
When in His strength I struggle,
  For very joy I leap,
When in my sin I totter,
  I weep, or try to weep:
But grace, sweet grace celestial,
  Shall all its love display,
And David's Royal Fountain
  Purge every sin away.

42.

O mine, my golden Syon!
  O lovelier far than gold,
With laurel-girt battalions,
  And safe victorious fold!
O sweet and blessed Country,
  Shall I ever see thy face?
O sweet and blessed Country,
  Shall I ever win thy grace?
I have the hope within me
  To comfort and to bless!
Shall I ever win the prize itself?
  O tell me, tell me, Yes!

43.

Exult, O duſt and aſhes!
The Lord *ſhall be thy part;*
His only, His for ever,
Thou ſhalt be, and thou art!
Exult, O duſt and aſhes!
The Lord *ſhall be thy part;*
His only, His for ever,
Thou ſhalt be, and thou art![9]

HORA NOVISSIMA.

BERNARD OF CLUNI.

HORA novissima, tempora pessima sunt, vigilemus.
Ecce minaciter imminet arbiter ille supremus.
Imminet, imminet et mala terminet, æqua coronet,
Recta remuneret, anxia liberet, æthera donet,
Auferat aspera duraque pondera mentes onustæ,
Sobria muniat, improba puniat, utraque juste.

* * * * *

Hic breve vivitur, hic breve plangitur, hic breve fletur;
Non breve vivere, non breve plangere retribuetur;
O retributio! stat brevis actio, vita perennis;
O retributio! cœlica mansio stat lue plenis;
Quid datur et quibus? æther egentibus et cruce dignis,
Sidera vermibus, optima sontibus, astra malignis.

Sunt modò prælia, poſtmodò præmia; qualia? plena,
Plena refectio, nullaque paſſio, nullaque pœna:
Spe modò vivitur, et Syon angitur a Babylone;
Nunc tribulatio; tunc recreatio, ſceptra, coronæ;
Tunc nova gloria pectora ſobria clarificabit,
Solvet enigmata, veraque ſabbata continuabit.
Liber et hoſtibus, et dominantibus ibit Hebræus;
Liber habebitur et celebrabitur hinc jubilæus.
Patria luminis, inſcia turbinis, inſcia litis,
Cive replebitur, amplificabitur Iſraëlitis;
Patria ſplendida, terraque florida, libera ſpinis,
Danda fidelibus eſt ibi civibus, hic peregrinis.
Tunc erit omnibus inſpicientibus ora Tonantis
Summa potentia, plena ſcientia, pax pia ſanctis;
Pax ſine crimine, pax ſine turbine, pax ſine rixa,
Meta laboribus, atque tumultibus anchora fixa.
Pars mea Rex meus, in proprio Deus ipſe decore
Viſus amabitur, atque videbitur Auctor in ore.
Tunc Jacob Iſraël, et Lia tunc Rachel efficietur,
Tunc Syon atria pulcraque patria perficietur.

O bona Patria, lumina ſobria te ſpeculantur,
Ad tua nomina lumina ſobria collacrymantur;

Est tua mentio pectoris unctio, cura doloris,
Concipientibus æthera mentibus ignis amoris.
Tu locus unicus, illeque cœlicus es paradisus,
Non ibi lacryma, sed placidissima gaudia, risus.
Est ibi consita laurus, et insita cedrus hysopo;
Sunt radiantia jaspide mænia, clara pyropo:
Hinc tibi sardius, inde topazius, hinc amethystus;
Est tua fabrica concio cœlica, gemmaque Christus.
Tu sine littore, tu sine tempore, fons modò rivus,
Dulce bonis sapis, estque tibi lapis undique vivus.
Est tibi laurea, dos datur aurea, sponsa decora,
Primaque Principis oscula suscipis, inspicis ora:
Candida lilia, viva monilia sunt tibi, Sponsa,
Agnus adest tibi, Sponsus adest tibi, lux speciosa:
Tota negocia, cantica dulcia dulce tonare,
Tam mala debita, quàm bona præbita conjubilare.
Urbs Syon aurea, patrea lactea, cive decora,
Omne cor obruis, omnibus obstruis et cor et ora.
Nescio, nescio, quæ jubilatio, lux tibi qualis,
Quàm socialia gaudia, gloria quàm specialis:
Laude studens ea tollere, mens mea victa fatiscit:

O bona gloria, vincor ; in omnia laus tua vicit.
Sunt Syon atria conjubilantia, martyre plena,
Cive micantia, Principe ſtantia, luce ſerena :
Eſt ibi paſcua, mitibus afflua, præſtita ſanctis,
Regis ibi thronus, agminis et ſonus eſt epulantis.
Gens duce ſplendida, concio candida veſtibus
albis
Sunt ſine fletibus in Syon ædibus, ædibus almis ;
Sunt ſine crimine, ſunt ſine turbine, ſunt ſine
lite
In Syon ædibus editioribus Iſraëlitæ.
Urbs Syon inclyta, gloria debita glorificandis,
Tu bona viſibus interioribus intima pandis :
Intima lumina, mentis acumina te ſpeculantur,
Pectora flammea ſpe modò, poſtea ſorte lucrantur.
Urbs Syon unica, manſio myſtica, condita cœlo,
Nunc tibi gaudeo, nunc mihi lugeo, triſtor,
anhelo :
Te quia corpore non queo, pectore ſæpe penetro,
Sed caro terrea, terraque carnea, mox cado
retro
Nemo retexere, nemoque promere ſuſtinet ore,
Quo tua mœnia, quo capitalia plena decore ;

Opprimit omne cor ille tuus decor, O Syon, O
pax,
Urbs ſine tempore, nulla poteſt fore laus tibi
mendax;
O ſine luxibus, O ſine luctibus, O ſine lite
Splendida curia, florida patria, patria vitæ!
Urbs Syon inclyta, turris et edita littore tuto,
Te peto, te colo, te flagro, te volo, canto, ſa-
luto;
Nec meritis peto, nam meritis meto morte
perire,
Nec reticens tego, quod meritis ego filius iræ;
Vita quidem mea, vita nimis rea, mortua vita,
Quippe reatibus exitialibus obruta, trita.
Spe tamen ambulo, præmia poſtulo ſpeque fide-
que,
Illa perennia poſtulo præmia nocte dieque.
Me Pater optimus atque piiſſimus ille creavit;
In lue pertulit, ex lue ſuſtulit, à lue lavit.
Gratia cœlica ſuſtinet unica totius orbis,
Parcere ſordibus, interioribus unctio morbis;
Diluit omina cœlica gratia, fons David undans
Omnia diluit, omnibus affluit, omnia mundans;
O pia gratia, celſa palatia cernere præſta,

Ut videam bona, feſtaque conſona, cœlica feſta.
O mea, ſpes mea, tu Syon aurea, clarior auro,
Agmine ſplendida, ſtans duce, florida perpete lauro,
O bona patria, num tua gaudia teque videbo?
O bona patria, num tua præmia plena tenebo?
Dic mihi, flagito, verbaque reddito, dicque, videbis.
Spem ſolidam gero; remne tenens ero? dic, Retinebis
O ſacer, O pius, O ter et amplius ille beatus,
Cui ſua pars Deus, O miſer, O reus hâc viduatus.

NOTES.

1 "Le ſurnom de Bernard varie en trois manières dans les manuſcrits. Les uns l'expriment par Morlanenſis qui Pitſeus rapporte à une ville d'Angleterre ſans la deſigner; les autres portent Morvalenſis, que Fabricius explique de la vallée de Maurienne; il en eſt enfin où l'on trouve Morlacenſis, qu'on peut appliquer ou à Morlaix en Baſſe-Bretagne, ou à la Morlas dans le comté de Bigorre. Mais il eſt certain, 1°, que la ſeconde dénomination eſt la plus rare; 2°, que les anciennes chartes emploient indifferemment les deux autres pour marquer un citoyen de la derniere ville, ce qui nous fait pencher à la regarder comme la vraie patrie de Bernard."—*Hiſtoire Littéraire de la France.*

Dr. Neale ſays that Bernard was "born at Morlaix in Bretagne, but of Engliſh parents." Trench calls him "the contemporary and fellow-countryman of his more illuſtrious nameſake of Clairvaux." Pitſeus ſimply ſays, "*Natione Angliis, ordinis S. Benedicti, Monachus Cluniacenſis.*"

2 In his introduction to "The Celeſtial Country," Dr. Neale ſays:—"I have here deviated from my ordinary rule of adopting the meaſure of the original; becauſe our language, if it could be tortured to any diſtant reſemblance of its rhythm, would utterly fail to give any idea of the majeſtic ſweetneſs of the Latin."—*Mediæval Hymns and Sequences.* London, 2d Edition.

3 "As a contraſt to the miſery and pollution of earth," ſays Dr. Neale, "the poem [*De Contemptu Mundi*] opens with a deſcription of the peace and glory of heaven, of ſuch rare beauty

as not eaſily to be matched by any mediæval compoſition on the ſame ſubject. Dean Trench, in his 'Sacred Latin Poetry,' gave a very beautiful cento of ninety-five lines from the work. From that cento I tranſlated the larger part in the firſt edition of the preſent book, following the arrangement of Dean Trench, and not that of Bernard. The great popularity which my tranſlation, however inferior to the original, attained, is evinced by the very numerous hymns compiled from it, which have found their way into modern collections; ſo that in ſome ſhape or other the Cluniac's verſes have become, as it were, naturalized among us. This led me to think that a fuller extract from the Latin, and a further tranſlation into Engliſh, might not be unacceptable to the lovers of ſacred poetry."

"It would be moſt unthankful did I not expreſs my gratitude to God for the favor He has given ſome of the centos made from the poem, but eſpecially *Jeruſalem the Golden.* It has found a place in ſome twenty hymnals; and for the laſt two years it has hardly been poſſible to read any newſpaper, which gives prominence to eccleſiaſtical news, without ſeeing its employment chronicled at ſome dedication or other feſtival. It is alſo a great favorite with diſſenters, and has obtained admiſſion to the Roman Catholic ſervices. 'And I ſay this,' to quote Bernard's own preface, 'in no wiſe arrogantly, but with all humility, and therefore boldly.'

"But more thankful ſtill am I that the Cluniac's verſes ſhould have ſoothed the dying hours of many of God's ſervants, the moſt ſtriking inſtance, of which I know, is related in the memoir publiſhed by Mr. Brownlow, under the title, *A Little Child ſhall lead them;* where he ſays that the child of whom he writes, when ſuffering agonies which the medical attendants declared to be almoſt unparalleled, would lie without a murmur or motion, while the whole four hundred lines were read.

"I have no heſitation in ſaying that I look on theſe verſes of Bernard as the moſt lovely, in the ſame way that the *Dies Iræ* is the moſt ſublime, and the *Stabat Mater* the moſt pathetic of mediæval poems. They are even ſuperior to that glorious hymn on the ſame ſubject, the *De Gloriâ et Gaudiis Paradiſi* of St. Peter Damiani. For the ſake of compariſon, I quote ſome of the moſt ſtriking ſtanzas of the latter, availing myſelf of the admirable tranſlation of Mr. Wackerbarth (*Med. Hymns*, 2d Edition, London):

THE GLORY AND JOYS OF PARADISE.

THERE nor waxing moon, nor waning
　Sun nor ſtars in courſes bright;
For the LAMB to that glad city
　Shines an everlaſting light:
There the daylight beams for ever,
　All unknown are time and night.

For the Saints, in beauty beaming,
　Shine in light and glory pure;
Crowned in triumph's fluſhing honors,
　Joy in uniſon ſecure;
And in ſafety tell their battles,
　And their foes' diſcomfiture.

Freed from every ſtain of evil,
　All their carnal wars are done;
For the fleſh made ſpiritual
　And the ſoul agree in one;
Peace unbroken ſpreads enjoyment,
　Sin and ſcandal are unknown.

Here they live in endleſs being;
Paſſingneſs hath paſſed away;
Here they bloom, they thrive, they flouriſh,
For decayed is all decay:
Laſting energy hath ſwallowed
Darkling death's malignant ſway.

Though each one's reſpective merit
Hath its varying palm aſſigned,
Love takes all as his poſſeſſion,
Where his power hath all combined;
So that all that each poſſeſſes
All partake in unconfined.

CHRIST, Thy ſoldiers' palm of honor,
Unto this Thy city free
Lead me when my warfare's girdle
I ſhall caſt away from me—
A partaker in Thy bounty
With Thy bleſſed ones to be.

Grant me vigor, while I labor
In the ceaſeleſs battle preſſed,
That Thou mayſt, the conflict over,
Grant me everlaſting reſt;
And I may at length inherit
Thee, my portion ever bleſt."

"Archdeacon Trench ſays very well, after referring to the Ode of Caſimir (the great Latin poet of Poland), *Urit me Patriæ decor*, that both 'turn upon the ſame theme, the heavenly home-ſickneſs; but with all the claſſical beauty of the Ode, and it is great, who does not feel that the poor Cluniac monk's is the more real and deep utterance?'

"The Ode, however, is well worthy of a translation, and here is an attempt:

IT KINDLES ALL MY SOUL.

It kindles all my soul,
My Country's loveliness! Those starry choirs
That watch around the pole,
And the moon's tender light, and heavenly fires
Through golden halls that roll.
O chorus of the night! O planets, sworn
The music of the spheres
To follow! Lovely watchers, that think scorn
To rest till day appears!
Me, for celestial homes of glory born,
Why here, oh why so long,
Do ye behold an exile from on high?
Here, O ye shining throng,
With lilies spread the mound where I shall lie:
Here let me drop my chain,
And dust to dust returning, cast away
The trammels that remain;
The rest of me shall spring to endless day!"

4 These two lines are taken from the last London edition. In some editions they are thus given:

"And the perfect from the shattered,
And the fallen from them that stand."

5 "Leah and Rachel are allegorized in three different ways by mediæval poets. First, of the active and contemplative life; and

thence alſo, by an eaſy tranſition, to the toil we endure on earth, and the eternal contemplation of God's glory in Heaven as here. So again, in a fine but rugged proſe in the Nuremberg Miſſal for St. Jerome's Day:

Then, when all carnal ſtrife hath ceaſed,
And we from warfare are releaſed,
O grant us in that Heavenly Feaſt
  To ſee Thee as Thou art:
To Leah give, the battle won,
  Her Rachel's dearer heart;
To Martha, when the ſtrife is done,
  Her Mary's better part.

"The parallel ſymbol of Martha and Mary is, however, in this ſenſe far more common, and is even found in epitaphs, as in that of Gundreda de Warren, daughter of William the Conqueror:

A Martha to the houſeleſs poor, a Mary in her love;
And though her Martha's part be gone, her Mary's lives above.

"Bernard, in the paſſage we are conſidering, has a double propriety in the changes of which he ſpeaks. Iſrael, according to St. Auguſtine's rendering, means, *He that beholds God;* Rachel, according to the unwarrantable mediæval explanation, *That beholds the Beginning, i. e.*, CHRIST. Thus, the change ſpoken of is from earth to the Beatific Viſion; and has a reference alſo to the New Name and White Stone of the Apocalypſe.

"The ſecond allegory of Leah and Rachel expounds them of the Synagogue and the Church; the third makes them to repreſent earthly affliction patiently endured"—*Mediæval Hymns.* 2d Edition.

6 "It is not without a deep mystical meaning that these stones are selected by the poet.

"The twelve foundation stones of the Apocalypse gave rise, as might be expected, to an infinite variety of mystical interpretations. 'Jasper,' says the comment of Marbodus, 'is the first foundation of the Church of God, and is of a green color.' 'It signifies those who always hold the Faith of God and never depart from it, or wither, but are always flourishing therein, and fear not the assaults of the devil.' 'The emerald is exceeding green, surpassing all gems and herbs in greenness.' 'By the emerald we understand those who excel others in the vigor of their faith, and dwell among infidels who be frigid and arid in their love.' 'The sardius, which is wholly red, signifies the martyrs who pour forth their blood for CHRIST.' 'The topaz is rare, and therefore precious. It has two colors, one like gold, the other clearer. In clearness it surpasses all gems, and nothing is more beautiful. It signifies those who love God and their neighbor.' 'The amethyst is entirely red, and shoots out rosy flames. Its color signifies earthly suffering; its emissions, prayers for those that cause it.'" —*Mediæval Hymns.* 2d Edition.

7 These stanzas are evidently considered by Dr. Neale his best. See page 37. *In deference to that opinion*, they are given here in the form in which they appear in the last edition of *Mediæval Hymns*.

8 "*Decachord*, with reference to the mystical explanation, which, seeing in the number *ten* a type of perfection, understands the 'instrument of ten strings' of the perfect harmony of heaven."

9 "I have been so often asked to what tune the words of Bernard may be sung, that I may here mention that of Mr. Ewing, the earliest written, the best known, and with children the most

popular; that of my friend, the Rev. H. L. Jenner, perhaps the moſt eccleſiaſtical; and that of another friend, Mr. Edmund Sedding, which, to my mind, beſt expreſſes the meaning of the words."—*Mediæval Hymns.* 2d Edition.

10 No copy of *De Contemptu Mundi* is known to be in the United States, and hence the extract given is only the cento from Trench's *Sacred Latin Poetry*, preceded by the firſt ſix lines of the poem. It is the part firſt tranſlated by Dr. Neale, beginning at the line, "Brief life is here our portion."

NOTE, that in this edition of *The Celeſtial Country* theſe changes have been made:

1ſt. The poem has been divided into irregular ſtanzas. This change of form is partly for the convenience of thoſe who love to refer and re-refer to favorite paſſages; partly to enable children readily to ſelect from it ſtanzas to be learned or ſung; but chiefly to render its intermingling ſentences more clear to thoſe who have not become familiar with its conſtruction.

2d. The punctuation has been materially remodelled and changed.

3d. The author's text has been altered in three inſtances, wherein the errors corrected ſeem manifeſtly ſlips of the pen or blunders of the compoſitor, viz., in the ninth ſtanza, line fourteen, "thoſe" is ſubſtituted for "them;" in the twenty-ſecond ſtanza, line two, "Thy" is ſubſtituted for "His," and in the forty-firſt ſtanza, line nine, "But" is ſubſtituted for "And."

THE DIES IRÆ.

A FRANCISCAN monk named Thomas, born near the beginning of the thirteenth century, at Celano, a Neapolitan village, achieved ſome reputation in his time as the friend and biographer of St. Francis de Aſſiſi, founder of the Order of Minorites. About the year 1250, as is ſuppoſed, he wrote a brief lyric, which, reaching above and beyond his creed and time, has entered in ſome form into the worſhip of every Chriſtian people. In the Romiſh Burial Service it forms the *Sequence for the Dead*, and is ſung with ſolemn majeſty at the great Sixtine Chapel, while portions of it enter into the praiſe or meditations of nearly "all who profeſs and call themſelves Chriſtians." So that, becoming more highly eſteemed, and more generally known with each century of its long hiſtory, it is at the preſent time both ſung at Rome and approved by all Proteſtant Chriſtendom.

A long lift might be framed of the great who have avowed for it a fupreme admiration, excelling that yielded to any other compofition of its kind. And fuch a roll would contain the names of men of different countries as of different creeds; of foldiers, ftatefmen and poets; of hiftorians, Churchmen, and compofers, upon whofe lips it has hovered, and in whofe works it has been engraved. Mozart, Haydn, Goethe, Schlegel, Johnfon, Dryden, Scott, Milman, and Jeremy Taylor would be among thefe names.

This lyric, which is the greateft of hymns, neverthelefs is caft in the fimpleft of forms. Beginning with an exclamation from the Scriptures, it continues through its few ftanzas the addrefs of a fingle actor upon a fingle fubject. Its meafure could not be more artlefs, nor its ftanzas more fimple. The auguft language in which it is clothed, it has bent into the form of rhyme, and this rhyme is of a kind which is faid to be wanting in dignity, and better adapted to comic than to elevated verfe. Yet it commands the homage of the Englifhman, the German, the Italian, and the modern Greek;

and even poſſeſſes ſo ſtrange a gift of faſcination, a gift in which no other compoſition equals and but one other approaches it, that the very ſound of its words will allure him who is ignorant of their meaning.

This marvellous power cannot be meaſured and defined, yet a diſtinguiſhed American clergyman has thus cloſely analyzed it: "Combining ſomewhat of the rhythm of claſſical "Latin, with the rhymes of the mediæval Latin, "treating of a theme full of awful ſublimity, and "grouping together the moſt ſtartling imagery of "Scripture as to the laſt Judgment, and throwing "this into yet ſtronger relief by the barbaric ſim-"plicity of the ſtyle in which it is ſet, and adding "to all theſe its full and trumpet-like cadences, "and uniting with the impaſſioned feelings of the "South, whence it emanated, the gravity of the "North, whoſe ſeverer ſtyle it adopted."—*Dr. W. R. Williams.*

The Great Hymn has ever allured and eluded tranſlators. Its apparent artleſſneſs and ſimplicity indicate that it can be turned readily into another language, but its ſecret power refuſes to be thus transferred. A German theologian (Lifco, Berlin, 1843) has collected and publifhed eighty-feven verfions, nearly all of which are in the German. In our Englifh tongue the tafk of rendering the Latin into verfe of the fame meafure is more difficult, and fome of our tranflators have fought to reproduce the form, and others to preferve the power of the original. The reader of Scott will remember with what ftrength a few ftanzas burft on us in the firft reading of "The Lay." In form and meaning they hardly claim the name of a tranflation, yet they have caught the fpirit of the hymn with a vividnefs that nothing in our language equals.

The mafs was fung, and prayers were faid,
And folemn requiem for the dead;
And bells toll'd out their mighty peal,
For the departed fpirit's weal;
And ever in the office clofe
The hymn of interceffion rofe;
And far the echoing aifles prolong
The awful burden of the fong—
　　DIES IRÆ, DIES ILLA!
　　SOLVET SÆCLUM IN FAVILLA;

While the pealing organ rung ;
  Were it meet with ſacred ſtrain
  To cloſe my lay ſo light and vain,
Thus the holy Fathers ſung :

That day of wrath, that dreadful day !
When heaven and earth ſhall paſs away,
What power ſhall be the ſinner's ſtay ?
How ſhall he meet that dreadful day ?

When ſhrivelling like a parchèd ſcroll
The flaming heavens together roll ;
When louder yet, and yet more dread,
Swells the high trump that wakes the dead !

Oh ! on that day, that wrathful day
When man to judgment wakes from clay,
Be Thou the trembling ſinner's ſtay,
Though heaven and earth ſhall paſs away !

I.

The eſtabliſhed verſion of the hymn is known as that of Paris. It differs in but one line from that of Rome, which has for the third line of the firſt ſtanza, *Crucis expandens vexilla.*

There have been ſtanzas prefixed to the hymn and others added; but, in its great ſtrength, it has ſhaken off all ſuch ſpurious additions. A marble ſlab in the Church of St. Francis, at Mantua, bore a copy of the hymn prefaced by five ſtanzas, which many ſcholars have thought, from the great age of the church, authentic. But the church is a century younger than the hymn, and theſe ſtanzas condemn themſelves:

Dies illa, dies iræ
Quam conemur prævenire,
Obveamque Deo iræ.

The inverſion of the Scriptural text, the poverty of the rhyme, and the weakneſs of the thought, are not faults of the DIES IRÆ. Its author undoubtedly took the quotation from Zephaniah as a text, and placed it at the head of his compoſition; and the inverſion, "*Dies illa, dies iræ*," is the play upon words to which an imitator alone would reſort.

II.

The author of the firſt tranſlation given in this volume, in a preface to his work, ſays:

"A production univerſally acknowledged to "have no ſuperior of its class ſhould be as lit- "erally rendered as the ſtructure of the lan- "guage into which it is tranſlated will admit. "Moreover, no tranſlation can be complete "which does not conform to the original in its "rhythmic quantities. The muſic of the Dies "Iræ is as old as the hymn, if not older; and "with thoſe who are familiar with both, they "are inſeparably connected in thought. To "ſatisfy the exactions of ſuch minds, the ca- "dences muſt be the ſame."

In this endeavor the author has ſo well ſucceeded, that when this verſion is compared ſtanza by ſtanza with the original, it will be found to be in the ſame trochaic meaſure, in the ſame difficult double rhyme, in ſtanzas of the ſame triplicate conſtruction, and, with feweſt errors, to be as a tranſlation the moſt literal and juſt that has been made. Yet this ſucceſs in letters was achieved by a ſoldier, during the gloomieſt period of a great and diſtracting war. The author is Major-General John A. Dix, U. S. V., and the tranſlation was made at Fortreſs Monroe, in the ſecond year of the Rebellion.

III.

The intenſe power of the Great Hymn is alſo exemplified in the different renderings which have been made by the ſame author. Dr. Abraham Coles, an American phyſician, has performed indeed the remarkable taſk of making thirteen different verſions; ſix of which are in the trochaic meaſure and double rhyme of the hymn, and all are ſufficiently diſtinct and original to form the creditable work of thirteen different men. This verſion is the firſt of Dr. Coles.

IV.

The next version is the eleventh of Dr. Coles. It is in single rhyme and iambic verse, and therein differs from the original.

V.

This version is by that nobleman of whom Pope has written:

> "Such was Roscommon, not more learned than good,
> Of manners generous as his noble blood:
> To him the wit of Greece and Rome was known,
> And every author's merit but his own."

And of whom Dryden has confessed:

"It was my Lord Roscommon's essay on "translated verse which made me uneasy till I "tried whether or no I was capable of follow- "ing his rules, and of reducing the speculation "into practice."

And of whom Johnson has recorded:

"At the moment in which he expired, he "uttered, with an energy of voice that expressed

"the moſt fervent devotion, two lines of his
"own verſion of DIES IRÆ:

> 'My God, my Father, and my Friend,
> Do not forſake me in my end.'"

In the beautiful fervor of its devotion, Roſcommon's excels all other tranſlations, but its verſe is not that of the DIES IRÆ.

VI.

Craſhaw, the contemporary of Herbert, and friend of Cowley, is the author of this verſion. It is the oldeſt in our language (1646), though there is a weak paraphraſe by Drummond of Hawthornden, beginning:

> Ah, ſilly ſoul! what wilt thou ſay
> When He, whom heaven and earth obey,
> Comes man to judge in the laſt day!

No tranſlation ſurpaſſes Craſhaw's in ſtrength, but the form of his ſtanza and the meaſure of his verſe are leaſt like thoſe of the original.

VII.

The verſion of Dr. W. J. Irons may be regarded as the accepted verſion of the preſent day in Great Britain, and is the one ſelected by the *Hymnal Noted.* It is in the double rhyme and meaſure of the original, and parts of it bear a ſtriking reſemblance to the American verſion of General Dix. But a much more curious coincidence in conception, with an abſolute identity of language in many parts, exiſts in the unpubliſhed verſion of an accompliſhed tranſlator (Mr. A. Périès, of Philadelphia), wherein ſeveral ſtanzas differ but little from thoſe of General Dix. The eleventh ſtands as follows:

"Righteous Judge of retribution,
Grant us ſinners abſolution
Ere the day of diſſolution!"

VIII.

It is a notable fact in the hiſtory of the Dies Iræ, that the beſt Engliſh tranſlations which we poſſeſs are not the work of our great poets. A recent verſion, which ſo capable and accompliſhed a critic as Mr. Prime pronounces to be "in many reſpects the beſt Engliſh verſion hitherto produced, and peculiarly valuable for thoſe who do not read the Latin, and who deſire to gain ſome idea of the power and beauty of this moſt celebrated hymn of the Church," alſo illuſtrates this remarkable fact. The author is Edward Sloſſon, Eſq., of the bar of New York.

And in this connection it may be obſerved, that even ſo accompliſhed a maſter in proſe and verſe as Macaulay has ſucceeded no better in the difficult taſk than is ſhown by his verſion written for the London *Chriſtian Obſerver* in 1826, beginning—

"On that great, that awful day,
This vain world ſhall paſs away.
Thus the Sibyl ſang of old;
Thus hath holy David told.
There ſhall be a deadly fear
When the Avenger ſhall appear;
And, unveiled before his eye,
All the works of men ſhall lie."

I.

THOMAS DE CELANO.

Dies iræ, dies illa, dies tribulationis et anguſtiæ, dies calamitatis et miſeriæ, dies tenebrarum et caliginis, dies nebulæ et turbinis, dies tubæ et clangoris ſuper civitatis munitas, et ſuper angulos excelſos!—*Sophonia*, i. 15, 16.

I.

Dies iræ, dies illa!
Solvet ſæclum in favillâ,
Teſte David cum Sybillâ.

II.

Quantus tremor eſt futurus,
Quando Judex eſt venturus,
Cuncta ſtricte diſcuſſurus.

III.

Tuba mirum ſpargens ſonum
Per ſepulcra regionum,
Coget omnes ante thronum.

II.

GENERAL DIX.

THAT DAY, A DAY OF WRATH, *a day of trouble and diſtreſs, a day of waſteneſs and deſolation, a day of darkneſs and gloomineſs, a day of clouds and thick darkneſs, a day of the trumpet and alarm againſt the fenced cities, and againſt the high towers!*—ZEPHANIAH, i. 15, 16.

1.

DAY of vengeance, without morrow!
Earth ſhall end in flame and ſorrow,
As from Saint and Seer we borrow.

2.

Ah! what terror is impending,
When the Judge is ſeen deſcending,
And each ſecret veil is rending.

3.

To the throne, the trumpet ſounding,
Through the ſepulchres reſounding,
Summons all, with voice aſtounding.

IV.

Mors ſtupebit, et natura,
Quum reſurget creatura,
Judicanti reſponſura.

V.

Liber ſcriptus proferetur,
In quo totum continetur,
Unde mundus judicetur.

VI.

Judex ergo cum ſedebit,
Quidquid latet, apparebit :
Nil inultum remanebit.

VII.

Quid ſum, miſer ! tunc dicturus,
Quem patronum rogaturus,
Quum vix juſtus ſit ſecurus ?

4.

Death and Nature, mazed, are quaking,
When, the grave's long ſlúmber breaking,
Man to judgment is awaking.

5.

On the written Volume's pages,
Life is ſhown in all its ſtages—
Judgment-record of paſt ages!

6.

Sits the Judge, the raiſed arraigning,
Darkeſt myſteries explaining,
Nothing unavenged remaining.

7.

What ſhall I then ſay, unfriended,
By no advocate attended,
When the juſt are ſcarce defended?

VIII.

Rex tremendæ majeſtatis,
Qui ſalvandos ſalvas gratis,
Salva me, fons pietatis!

IX.

Recordare, Jeſu pie,
Quod ſum cauſa tuæ viæ;
Ne me perdas illâ die!

X.

Quærens me, ſediſti laſſus,
Redemiſti, crucem paſſus:
Tantus labor non ſit caſſus.

XI.

Juſte Judex ultionis,
Donum fac remiſſionis
Ante diem rationis.

8.

King of majeſty tremendous,
By Thy ſaving grace defend us,
Fount of pity, ſafety ſend us!

9.

Holy JESUS, meek, forbearing,
For my ſins the death-crown wearing,
Save me, in that day, deſpairing.

10.

Worn and weary, Thou haſt ſought me;
By Thy croſs and paſſion bought me—
Spare the hope Thy labors brought me.

11.

Righteous Judge of retribution,
Give, O give me abſolution
Ere the day of diſſolution.

XII.

Ingemiſco tanquam reus,
Culpâ rubet vultus meus ;
Supplicanti parce, Deus !

XIII.

Qui Mariam abſolviſti,
Et latronem exaudiſti,
Mihi quoque ſpem dediſti.

XIV.

Preces meæ non ſunt dignæ,
Sed Tu bonus fac benigne
Ne perenni cremer igne !

XV.

Inter oves locum præſta,
Et ab hædis me ſequeſtra,
Statuens in parte dextrâ.

12.

As a guilty culprit groaning,
Fluſhed my face, my errors owning,
Hear, O God, my ſpirit's moaning!

13.

Thou to Mary gav'ſt remiſſion,
Heard'ſt the dying thief's petition,
Bad'ſt me hope in my contrition.

14.

In my prayers no grace diſcerning,
Yet on me Thy favor turning,
Save my ſoul from endleſs burning.

15.

Give me, when Thy ſheep confiding
Thou art from the goats dividing,
On Thy right a place abiding!

XVI.

Confutatis maledictis,
Flammis acribus addictis,
Voca me cum benedictis!

XVII.

Oro ſupplex et acclinis,
Cor contritum quaſi cinis,
Gere curam mei finis.

XVIII.

Lacrymoſa dies illa!
Qua reſurget ex favillâ.
Judicandus homo reus;
Huic ergo parce, Deus!

16.

When the wicked are confounded,
And by bitter flames ſurrounded,
Be my joyful pardon ſounded!

17.

Proſtrate, all my guilt diſcerning,
Heart as though to aſhes turning;
Save, O ſave me from the burning!

18.

Day of weeping, when from aſhes
Man ſhall riſe mid lightning flaſhes,
Guilty, trembling with contrition,
Save him, Father, from perdition!

III.

DR. COLES.

I.

DAY of wrath, that day of burning,
Seer and ſibyl ſpeak concerning,
All the world to aſhes turning.

2.

Oh, what fear ſhall it engender,
When the Judge ſhall come in ſplendor,
Strict to mark and juſt to render.

3.

Trumpet ſcattering ſounds of wonder,
Rending ſepulchres aſunder,
Shall reſiſtleſs ſummons thunder.

IV.

DR. COLES.

I.

DAY of wrath, that day of dole,
When a fire ſhall wrap the whole,
And the earth be burnt to coal!

2.

O, what horror ſmiting dumb
When the Judge of all ſhall come,
Sinful deeds to ſearch and ſum!

3.

Trump's reverberating roar
Through the ſepulchres ſhall pour,
Citing all the Throne before.

4.

All aghaſt then Death ſhall ſhiver,
And great Nature's frame ſhall quiver,
When the graves their dead deliver.

5.

Book where actions are recorded,
All the ages have afforded
Shall be brought, and dooms awarded.

6.

When ſhall ſit the Judge unerring,
He'll unfold all here occurring,
No juſt vengeance then deferring.

7.

What ſhall I ſay, that time pending?
Aſk what advocate's befriending,
When the juſt man needs defending?

4.

Death and Nature ſtand aghaſt,
While the dead, in numbers vaſt,
Riſe to anſwer for the paſt.

5.

Volume writ by God's own pen,
Chronicling the deeds of men,
Shall be brought, and dooms be then.

6.

When the Judge ſhall ſit, behold!
What is ſecret He'll unfold,
No juſt puniſhment withhold.

7.

Ah! what plea ſhall I prepare,
To what Patron make my prayer,
When the juſt well-nigh deſpair?

8.

Dreadful King, all power poſſeſſing,
Saving freely thoſe confeſſing,
Save Thou me, O Fount of Bleſſing!

9.

Think, O Jesus, for what reaſon
Thou didſt bear earth's ſpite and treaſon,
Nor me loſe in that dread ſeaſon!

10.

Seeking me Thy worn feet haſted,
On the croſs Thy ſoul death taſted:
Let ſuch travail not be waſted!

11.

Righteous Judge of retribution!
Make me gift of abſolution
Ere that day of execution!

8.

King majeſtic beyond thought,
Whoſe free grace cannot be bought,
Save me, whoſe deſert is naught!

9.

O remember, Jesus, I
Was the cauſe and reaſon why
Thou didſt come on earth to die!

10.

Me Thou ſought'ſt with weary feet,
And my ranſom didſt complete:
Let ſuch pity naught defeat!

11.

Judge inflexible and ſtrict,
Pardon, ere that day convict,
And th' unchanging doom inflict!

12.

Culprit-like I plead, heart-broken,
On my cheek ſhame's crimſon token:
Let the pardoning word be ſpoken!

13.

Thou who Mary gav'ſt remiſſion,
Heard'ſt the dying thief's petition,
Cheer'ſt with hope my loſt condition.

14.

Though my prayers be void of merit,
What is needful, Thou confer it,
Leſt I endleſs fire inherit!

15.

Be there, Lord, my place decided
With Thy ſheep, from goats divided,
Kindly to Thy right hand guided!

12.

Like a criminal I ſigh,
Bluſhing, penitently cry:
Paſs, Lord, my offences by!

13.

Thou, who Mary erſt didſt bleſs,
Heard'ſt the thief in his diſtreſs;
Hope has given me no leſs.

14.

Worthleſs are my prayers and vain,
But in love do not diſdain,
Leſt I reap eternal pain!

15.

On Thy right hand grant me place
Mid the ſheep, a choſen race—
Far from goats devoid of grace!

16.

When th' accurſed away are driven,
To eternal burnings given,
Call me with the bleſſed to heaven!

17.

I beſeech Thee, proſtrate lying,
Heart as aſhes, contrite, ſighing,
Care for me when I am dying!

18.

Day of tears and late repentance,
Man ſhall riſe to hear his ſentence:
Him, the child of guilt and error,
Spare, Lord, in that hour of terror!

16.

When the thunder of Thine ire
Headlong hurls to quenchleſs fire,
Let Thy welcome me inſpire!

17.

I entreat Thee, bending low,
Heart as aſhes, full of woe,
Succor in mine end beſtow!

18.

When upon that day of tears
Man from duſt again appears,
Fate depending on Thy nod:
Spare the ſinner then, O God!

V.

EARL ROSCOMMON.

I.

THE day of wrath, that dreadful day,
Shall the whole world in ashes lay,
As David and the Sibyls say.

2.

What horror will invade the mind
When the strict Judge, who would be kind,
Shall have few venial faults to find.

3.

The last loud trumpet's wondrous sound
Shall through the rending tombs rebound,
And wake the nations under ground.

VI.

RICHARD CRASHAW

I.

HEAR'ST thou, my ſoul, what ſerious things
Both the Pſalm and Sibyl ſings
Of a ſure Judge, from whoſe ſharp ray
The world in flames ſhall fly away!

2.

O that Fire! before whoſe face
Heaven and earth ſhall find no place:
O thoſe Eyes! whoſe angry light
Muſt be the day of that dread night.

3.

O that Trump! whoſe blaſt ſhall run
An even round with th' circling Sun,
And urge the murmuring graves to bring
Pale mankind forth to meet his King.

4.

Nature and death ſhall with ſurpriſe
Behold the pale offender riſe,
And view the Judge with conſcious eyes.

5.

Then ſhall, with univerſal dread,
The ſacred, myſtic book be read
To try the living and the dead.

6.

The Judge aſcends His awful throne;
He makes each ſecret ſin be known,
And all with ſhame confeſs their own.

7.

O then, what intereſt ſhall I make
To ſave my laſt important ſtake
When the moſt juſt have cauſe to quake!

4.

Horror of Nature, Hell, and Death!
When a deep groan from beneath
Shall cry, "We come, we come!" and all
The caves of night anſwer one call.

5.

O that book! whoſe leaves ſo bright
Will ſet the world in ſevere light.
O that Judge! whoſe hand, whoſe eye
None can endure, yet none can fly.

6.

Ah then, poor ſoul! what wilt thou ſay?
And to what patron chooſe to pray,
When ſtars themſelves ſhall ſtagger, and
The moſt firm foot no more ſhall ſtand?

7.

But Thou giv'ſt leave, dread Lord, that we
Take ſhelter from Thyſelf in Thee;
And with the wings of Thine own dove
Fly to Thy ſceptre of ſoft love!

8.

Thou mighty, formidable King!
Thou mercy's unexhausted spring,
Some comfortable pity bring!

9.

Forget not what my ransom cost;
Nor let my dear-bought soul be lost,
In storms of guilty terrors tost.

10.

Thou who for me didst feel such pain,
Whose precious blood the cross did stain,
Let not these agonies be vain!

11.

Thou whom avenging powers obey,
Cancel my debt, too great to pay,
Before the sad accounting day!

8.

Dear [Lord], remember in that day
Who was the cauſe Thou cam'ſt this way;
Thy ſheep was ſtrayed, and Thou wouldſt be
Even loſt Thyſelf in ſeeking me!

9.

Shall all that labor, all that coſt
Of love, and even that loſs, be loſt?
And this loved ſoul judged worth no leſs
Than all that way and wearineſs?

10.

Juſt Mercy, then, Thy reck'ning be
With my price, and not with me;
'Twas paid at firſt with too much pain
To be paid twice, or once in vain.

11.

Mercy, my Judge, mercy I cry,
With bluſhing cheek and bleeding eye;
The conſcious colors of my ſin
Are red without, and pale within.

12.

Surrounded with amazing fears,
Whoſe load my ſoul with anguiſh bears,
I ſigh, I weep! accept my tears!

13.

Thou who wert moved with Mary's grief,
And by abſolving of the thief
Haſt given me hope, now give relief!

14.

Reject not my unworthy prayer;
Preſerve me from the dangerous ſnare
Which death and gaping hell prepare.

15.

Give my exalted ſoul a place
Among Thy choſen right-hand race,
The ſons of God and heirs of grace.

12.

O let Thine own ſoft bowels pay
Thyſelf, and ſo diſcharge that day!
If Sin can ſigh, Love can fórgive,
O, ſay the word, my ſoul ſhall live!

13.

Thoſe mercies which Thy Mary found,
Or who Thy croſs confeſs'd and crowned,
Hope tells my heart the ſame loves be
Still alive, and ſtill for me.

14.

Though both my prayers and tears combine,
Both worthleſs are, for they are mine;
But Thou Thy bounteous ſelf ſtill be,
And ſhow Thou art by ſaving me.

15.

O when Thy laſt frown ſhall proclaim
The flocks of goats to folds of flame,
And all Thy loſt ſheep found ſhall be,
Let "Come ye bleſſed" then call me!

16.

From that inſatiable abyſs,
Where flames devour and ſerpents hiſs,
Promote me to thy ſeat of bliſs.

17.

Proſtrate my contrite heart I rend,
My God, my Father, and my Friend:
Do not forſake me in my end!

18.

Well may they curſe their ſecond breath
Who riſe to a reviving death:
Thou great Creator of mankind,
Let guilty man compaſſion find!

16.

When the dread "*ITE*" ſhall divide
Thoſe limbs of death from Thy left ſide,
Let thoſe life-ſpeaking lips command
That I inherit Thy right hand!

17.

O, hear a ſuppliant heart all cruſh'd,
And crumbled into contrite duſt!
My hope, my fear—my Judge, my Friend!
Take charge of me, and of my end!

VII.

DR. IRONS.

1.

DAY of Wrath! O Day of mourning!
See! once more the Croſs returning,
Heav'n and earth in aſhes burning!

2.

O what fear man's boſom rendeth,
When from Heav'n the Judge deſcendeth,
On whoſe ſentence all dependeth!

3.

Wondrous ſound the Trumpet flingeth,
Through earth's ſepulchres it ringeth,
All before the throne it bringeth!

VIII.

MR. SLOSSON.

I.

DAY OF WRATH! of days THAT DAY!
Earth in flames ſhall melt away,
Pſalmiſt thus and Sibyl ſay.

2.

What ſwift terrors then ſhall fall,
When deſcends the Judge of all,
Every action to recall!

3.

When the trump, with wondrous tone
Through the graves of nations gone,
Bids the race confront the Throne.

4.

Death is ſtruck, and nature quaking,
All creation is awaking,
To its Judge an anſwer making!

5.

Lo, the Book, exactly worded!
Wherein all hath been recorded;
Thence ſhall judgment be awarded.

6.

When the Judge His ſeat attaineth,
And each hidden deed arraigneth,
Nothing unaveng'd remaineth.

7.

What ſhall I, frail man, be pleading,
Who for me be interceding,
When the juſt are mercy needing?

4.

Death ſhall die—fair nature too;
As the creature, ris'n anew,
Anſwers to his God's review.

5.

HE the ſcroll of fate ſhall ſpread,
Writ with all things done or ſaid,
Thence to judge th' awaken'd dead.

6.

Lo! He takes His ſeat of light;
All that's dark ſhall leap to ſight,
Guilt, the ſword of vengeance ſmite.

7.

What can I, then, wretched, plead?
Who will mediate in my need
When the juſt ſhall ſcarce ſucceed?

8.

King of majeſty tremendous,
Who doſt free ſalvation ſend us,
Fount of pity ! then befriend us !

9.

Think ! Kind Jeſu, my ſalvation
Caus'd Thy wondrous Incarnation ;
Leave me not to reprobation !

10.

Faint and weary Thou haſt ſought me,
On the Croſs of ſuffering bought me ;
Shall ſuch grace be vainly brought me !

11.

Righteous Judge of retribution,
Grant Thy gift of abſolution,
Ere that reck'ning day's concluſion !

8.

King majeſtic! Sovereign dread!
Saving all for whom He bled,
Save Thou me! Salvation's Head!

9.

Holy Jeſus! priceleſs ſtay!
Think! for *me* Thy bleeding way!
Loſe me not, upon That Day.

10.

Faint and weary, Thou haſt ſought,
By the Croſs, my crown haſt bought;
Can ſuch anguiſh be for naught?

11.

Oh! Avenging Judge ſevere,
Grant remiſſion, full and clear,
Ere th' accounting day appear.

12.

Guilty, now I pour my moaning,
All my ſhame with anguiſh owning;
Spare, O God, Thy ſuppliant, groaning!

13.

Thou, the ſinful woman ſaveſt,
Thou, the dying thief forgaveſt;
And to me a hope vouchſafeſt!

14.

Worthleſs are my pray'rs and ſighing,
Yet, good Lord, in grace complying,
Reſcue me from fires undying!

15.

With Thy favor'd ſheep, O place me!
Nor among the goats abaſe me;
But to Thy right hand upraiſe me.

12.

Like a guilty thing I moan,
Flufh'd my cheek, my fins I own,
Hear, O God, Thy fuppliant's groan!

13.

Magdalen found grace with Thee,
So the thief upon the tree;
Hope Thou giveft e'en to me.

14.

Worthlefs are my vows, I know,
Yet, dear Lord, Thy pity fhow,
Left I fink in endlefs woe.

15.

From the goats my lot divide,
With Thy lambs a place provide,
On Thy right and near Thy fide.

16.

While the wicked are confounded,
Doom'd to flames of woe unbounded,
Call me! with Thy ſaints ſurrounded.

17.

Low I kneel, with heart ſubmiſſion;
See, like aſhes, my contrition;
Help me, in my laſt condition!

18.

Ah! that Day of tears and mourning!
From the duſt of earth returning,
Man for judgment muſt prepare him;
Spare! O God, in mercy, ſpare him!

Lord, who didſt our ſouls redeem,
Grant a bleſſed Requiem! Amen.

16.

When th' accursèd ſink in ſhame,
Given to tormenting flame,
With Thy bleſſed call my name.

17.

Bowed to earth, I ſtrive in prayer;
Heart like cinders, ſee, I bear;
Its laſt throbbing be Thy care!

18.

AH! THAT DAY of burning tears,
When from aſhes reappears
Man all guilt, his doom to bear—
SPARE HIM, GOD! IN MERCY, SPARE!

THE STABAT MATER.

THE Stabat Mater, with the *Dies Iræ*, poſſeſſes the power of imparting a ſhadowy impreſſion of its meaning by the melody of its verſe. Its ſoft, ſad cadence echoes the feeling of its pathetic words. In fame it ranks next to the *Dies Iræ*, yet is neither ſo ſimple nor ſo grand; nor does it riſe, like the Great Hymn, above ſectarian faults. It has attracted the ſame great admiration, and been praiſed and repeated by the ſame great admirers, but always in a leſſer degree. As the *Dies Iræ* has been pronounced the greateſt, ſo the Stabat Mater univerſally is deemed the moſt pathetic of hymns.

The life of its author was in fit keeping with its plaintive utterances. He was born at Todi, of the noble Italian houſe of Benedette, and roſe to diſtinction as a juriſt. A few years after the *Dies Iræ* was written (1268), he loſt his wife, and, broken-hearted, renounced the world to join, like Thomas of Celano, the Order of St. Francis. In the ardor of his devotion, he tried to atone by ſelf-ſought tortures not only for his own ſins, but, like our Saviour, for the ſins of others. At laſt his ſorrows ſank into inſanity and ended in death.

Dying about the time that Petrarch was born, and while Dante was ſtill a young man, his *Cantace Spirituali* mark the dawning day of the Italian language. In an old Venetian copy of theſe, the hiſtorian of the Franciſcans (Wadding) found a number of Latin poems, amongſt which was the Stabat Mater, and thus eſtabliſhed for the Order of St. Francis the honor of producing, within the ſame century, the two moſt celebrated of Latin hymns.

Few Engliſh verſions of the Stabat Mater have been made, and not one which ſtrictly preſerves its meaſure. That of Lord Lindſay is ſelected here as beſt expreſſing the pathos of the original.

STABAT MATER.

JACOBUS DE BENEDICTIS.

I.

STABAT Mater dolorosa,
Juxta crucem lacrymosa,
Dum pendebat filius.
Cujus animam gementem,
Contristatam et dolentem,
Pertransivit gladius.

II.

O quam tristis et afflicta,
Fuit illa benedicta
Mater unigeniti!
Quæ mœrebat et dolebat,
Pia mater, dum videbat
Nati pœnas inclyti.

THE STABAT MATER.

LORD LINDSAY.

I.

BY the Crofs, fad vigil keeping,
Stood the mournful mother weeping,
While on it the Saviour hung;
In that hour of deep diftrefs,
Pierced the fword of bitternefs
Through her heart with forrow wrung.

2.

Oh! how fad, how woe-begone
Was that ever-bleffed one,
Mother of the Son of God!
Oh! what bitter tears fhe fhed
Whilft before her JESUS bled
'Neath the Father's penal rod!

III.

Quis eſt homo qui non fleret,
Chriſti matrem ſi videret
In tanto ſupplicio?
Quis poſſet non contriſtari
Piam matrem contemplari
Dolentem cum filio?

IV.

Pro peccatis ſuæ gentis,
Vidit Jeſum in tormentis,
Et flagellis ſubditum.
Vidit ſuum dulcem natum,
Morientem, deſolatum,
Dum emiſit ſpiritum.

V.

Eia mater, fons amoris,
Me ſentire vim doloris
Fac, ut tecum lugeam.
Fac ut ardeat cor meum,
In amando Chriſtum Deum
Ut illi complaceam.

3.

Who's the man could view unmoved
CHRIST'S ſweet mother, whom HE loved,
In ſuch dire extremity?
Who his pitying tears withhold,
CHRIST'S ſweet mother to behold
Sharing in His agony?

4.

For the Father's broken law,
Mary thus the Saviour ſaw
Sport of human cruelties—
Saw her ſweet, her only Son,
God-forſaken and undone,
Die a ſinleſs ſacrifice!

5.

Mary mother, fount of love,
Make me ſhare thy ſorrow, move
All my ſoul to ſympathy!
Make my heart within me glow
With the love of JESUS—ſo
Shall I find acceptancy.

VI.

Sanĉta Mater, iſtud agas,
Crucifixi fige plagas
    Cordi meo valide.
Tui Nati vulnerati,
Tam dignati pro me pati,
    Pœnas mecum divide.

VII.

Fac me vere tecum flere,
Crucifixo condolere,
    Donec ego vixero.
Juxta crucem tecum ſtare,
Et tibi me ſociare
    In planĉtu deſidero.

VIII.

Virgo virginum præclara,
Mihi jam non ſis amara ;
    Fac me tecum plangere.
Fac ut portem Chriſti mortem
Paſſionis fac conſortem,
    Et plagas recolere.

6.

Print, O Mother, on my heart,
Deeply print the wounds, the ſmart
    Of my Saviour's chaſtiſement;
He who, to redeem my loſs,
Deigned to bleed upon the croſs—
    Make me ſhare His puniſhment.

7.

Ever with thee, at thy ſide,
'Neath the CHRIST, the Crucified,
    Mournful mother, let me be!
By the Croſs ſad vigil keeping,
Ever watchful, ever weeping,
    Thy companion conſtantly!

8.

Maid of maidens, undefiled,
Mother gracious, mother mild,
    Melt my heart to weep with thee!
Crown me with CHRIST's thorny wreath,
Make me conſort of His death,
    Sharer of His victory.

IX.

Fac me plagis vulnerari,
Fac me cruce inebriari,
    Et cruore filii.
Inflammatus et accensus,
Per te, Virgo, sim defensus,
    In die judicii.

X.

Fac me cruce custodiri,
Morte Christi præmuniri,
    Confoveri gratia.
Quando corpus morietur,
Fac ut animæ donetur
    Paradisi gloria.

9.

Never from the mingled tide
Flowing ſtill from Jesus' ſide,
May my lips inebriate turn;
And when in the day of doom,
Lightning-like He rends the tomb,
Shield, oh ſhield me, leſt I burn!

10.

So the ſhadow of the tree
Where thy Jesus bled for me
Still ſhall be my fortalice;
So when fleſh and ſpirit ſever
Shall I live, thy boon, for ever
In the joys of Paradiſe!

THE VENI SANCTE SPIRITUS.

IN the year 997, "whilſt the prieſthood ſtrug-
"gled to regain through their anathemas the "property that had been taken from them by "violence, a young man, who knew neither to "threaten nor to lie, nor to inſpire others with "fear, ſucceeded to the royal dignity which his "father had uſurped. It was Robert, only ſon "of Hugh Capet."—*Siſmondi*, *Hiſt. Français.*

This King, "there is no good reaſon to "doubt" (*Konigsfeld*), was the author of the VENI SANCTE SPIRITUS, a hymn that the beſt living authority regards as "the lovelieſt of all "the hymns in the whole circle of Latin ſacred "poetry."—*Trench.*

The ability of Robert II. to have compoſed the hymn which ranks next to the *Dies Iræ* and

Stabat Mater, is not improbable, for, according to the chronicle of Saint Bertin, he was a ſaint, a poet, and a muſician:

"Robert étoit très-pieux, prudent, lettré, et ſuffiſamment phi-
"loſophe, mais ſurtout excellent muſicien. Il compoſa la proſe
"du Saint-Eſprit, qui commence par ces mots, *Adſit nobis gratia*,
"les rhythmes, *Judæ et Hieruſalem*, et *Cornelius Centurio*, qu'il
"offrit à Rome ſur l'autel de Saint-Pierre, notés avec le chant
"qui leur étoit propre, de même que l'antiphone *Eripe*, et plu-
"ſieurs autres beaux morceaux."

The tranſlation which is here given is from the *Lyra Germanica* of Catherine Winkworth. That work profeſſes to be tranſlated from the German; but its verſion of the VENI SANCTE SPIRITUS is a finer tranſlation than any that profeſſes to be from the Latin.

The only alteration which has been made in the text is the firſt word of the Engliſh verſion. As there was no reaſon for rendering the Latin verb by the Engliſh interjection "O," it is preſumed that this was an unintended error of the uſually faithful and ſcrupulous tranſlator.

VENI SANCTE SPIRITUS.

ROBERT II.

I.

VENI, Sancte Spiritus,
Et emitte cœlitus,
Lucis tuæ radium.

II.

Veni, pater pauperum,
Veni, dator munerum,
Veni, lumen cordium.

III.

Consolator optime,
Dulcis hospes animæ,
Dulce refrigerium.

THE VENI SANCTE SPIRITUS.

CATHERINE WINKWORTH.

1.

COME, Holy Ghoſt! Thou fire divine!
From higheſt heaven on us down ſhine!
Comforter, be Thy comfort mine!

2.

Come, Father of the poor, to earth;
Come with Thy gifts of precious worth;
Come, Light of all of mortal birth!

3.

Thou rich in comfort! Ever bleſt
The heart where Thou art conſtant gueſt,
Who giv'ſt the heavy-laden reſt.

IV.

In labore requies,
In æstu temperies,
In fletu solatium.

V.

O lux beatissima!
Reple cordis intima,
Tuorum fidelium.

VI.

Sine tuo numine,
Nihil est in homine,
Nihil est innoxium.

VII.

Lava quod est sordidum,
Riga quod est aridum,
Sana quod est saucium.

4.

Come Thou in whom our toil is ſweet,
Our ſhadow in the noon-day heat,
Before whom mourning flieth fleet.

5.

Bright Sun of Grace! Thy ſunſhine dart
On all who cry to Thee apart,
And fill with gladneſs every heart.

6.

Whate'er without Thy aid is wrought,
Or ſkilful deed, or wiſeſt thought,
God counts it vain and merely naught.

7.

O cleanſe us that we ſin no more,
O'er parchèd ſouls Thy waters pour;
Heal the ſad heart that acheth ſore.

VIII.

Flecte quod eſt rigidum,
Fove quod eſt frigidum,
Rege quod eſt devium.

IX.

Da tuis fidelibus,
In te confidentibus,
Sacrum ſeptenarium.

X.

Da virtutis meritum,
Da ſalutis exitum,
Da perenne gaudium.

8.

Thy will be ours in all our ways;
O melt the frozen with Thy rays;
Call home the loſt in error's maze.

9.

And grant us, Lord, who cry to Thee,
And hold the Faith in unity,
Thy precious gifts of charity.

10.

That we may live in holineſs,
And find in death our happineſs,
And dwell with Thee in laſting bliſs!

THE VENI CREATOR SPIRITUS.

"CHARLEMAGNE, réclamé par l'Eglife comme un faint, par les Français comme "leur plus grand roi, par les Allemands comme "leur compatriote, par les Italiens comme leur "empereur," is the reputed author of this Latin hymn. Men naturally prefer to trace a venerable and renowned compofition to an unexpected authorfhip, and to find the refinement of letters in thofe otherwife diftinguifhed; ftill more, to difcover in a great foldier and a great king the doubly refined gift of *facred* poetry. It is not impoffible. "The eloquence of Charlemagne," fays his Secretary, "was abundant. "He was able to exprefs with facility all he "wifhed; and, not content with his mother-"tongue, he beftowed great pains upon foreign "languages. He had taken fo well to the Latin, "that he was able to fpeak publicly in that lan-

"guage almoſt as eaſily as in his own. He "underſtood Greek, and ſtudied Hebrew."

There remains of his muſe an epitaph on Adrian I., in thirty-eight verſes; the *Song of Roland*, an ode to the ſcholar Warnefride, and an epigram in hexameter verſe. This epigram was found in a manuſcript containing a commentary on the *Epiſtle to the Romans*, attributed to Origen, and corrected in the hand of Charlemagne. The ſubject of the hymn ſeems alſo to have engaged the attention of the Emperor, for there is a letter by him addreſſed to his biſhops, entitled *De gratia ſeptiformis Spiritus.* He died at Aix-la-Chapelle, his crown upon his head, and his copy of the Goſpels upon his knees, January 28, 814.

The Engliſh verſion of the hymn is the paraphraſe of Dryden, of which Warton ſays: "This "is a moſt elegant and beautiful little morſel, "and one of his moſt correct compoſitions." There is a tranſlation in the Prayer Book (Ordering of Prieſts) which is noteworthy, as being the only Breviary hymn retained by the Epiſcopal Church.

VENI CREATOR SPIRITUS.

CHARLEMAGNE.

VENI, Creator Spiritus,
Mentes tuorum visita,
Imple superna gratia,
Quæ tu creasti pectora.

Qui diceris Paraclitus,
Altissimi donum Dei,
Fons vivus, ignis, charitas,
Et spiritalis unctio.

Tu septiformis munere,
Digitus Paternæ dexteræ,
Tu rite promissum Patris,
Sermone ditans guttura.

Accende lumen sensibus,
Infunde amorem cordibus,
Infirma nostri corporis
Virtute firmans perpeti.

THE VENI CREATOR SPIRITUS.

DRYDEN.

CREATOR Spirit, by whofe aid
The world's foundations firft were laid,
Come vifit every pious mind,
Come pour Thy joys on human kind;
From fin and forrow fet us free,
And make Thy temples worthy Thee.

O SOURCE of uncreated light,
The Father's promifed Paraclete!
Thrice holy fount, thrice holy fire,
Our hearts with heavenly love infpire;
Come, and Thy facred unction bring,
To fanctify us while we fing.

PLENTEOUS of grace, defcend from high,
Rich in Thy fevenfold energy!
Thou ftrength of His almighty hand,
Whofe power does heaven and earth command.
Proceeding Spirit, our defence,
Who doft the gifts of tongues difpenfe,
And crown'ft Thy gift with eloquence!

Hoſtem repellas longius,
Pacemque dones protinus:
Duſtore ſic te prævio
Vitemus omne noxium.

Per te ſciamus da Patrem,
Noſcamus atque Filium;
Teque utriuſque Spiritum
Credamus omni tempore.

Deo Patri ſit gloria
Et Filio qui a mortuis
Surrexit, ac Paraclito,
In ſæculorum ſæcula.

REFINE and purge our earthly parts;
But, oh, inflame and fire our hearts!
Our frailties help, our vice control,
Submit the ſenſes to the ſoul;
And when rebellious they are grown,
Then lay Thy hand and hold 'em down.

CHASE from our minds th' infernal foe,
And peace the fruit of love beſtow;
And leſt our feet ſhould ſtep aſtray,
Protect and guide us on the way.

MAKE us eternal truths receive,
And practiſe all that we believe;
Give us Thyſelf, that we may ſee
The Father and the Son by Thee.

IMMORTAL honor, endleſs fame,
Attend the Almighty Father's name:
The Saviour Son be glorified,
Who for loſt man's redemption died;
And equal adoration be,
Eternal Paraclete, to Thee.

THE VEXILLA REGIS.

THE Vexilla Regis was written about the year 580—two hundred years before the time of Charlemagne, and seven hundred years before the birth of the English language. It is therefore one of the oldest of mediæval hymns.

Venantius Fortunatus, an Italian, whose birthplace is unknown, was in early life a citizen of Ravenna, from which he was driven by the great invasion of the Lombards. He passed into France, and became the fashionable poet of his time. Subsequently he devoted his talents to a holier object, and became the friend of Saint Radegunde and Saint Gregory. He removed to Tours, was made Bishop of Poitiers, and died about the year 600.

"This world-famous hymn, one of the grandeſt in the treaſury of the Latin Church, was compoſed by Fortunatus on occaſion of the reception of certain relics by Saint Gregory of Tours and Saint Radegunde, previouſly to the conſecration of a church at Poitiers. It is therefore ſtrictly and primarily a proceſſional hymn, though, very naturally, afterwards adapted to Paſſion-tide."—*Mediæval Hymns.*

"C'eſt de Fortunat qu'eſt le VEXILLA REGIS compoſé, à l'occaſion du morceau de la vraie croix, envoyé par l'empereur Juſtin à St. Radegonde."—*Biographie Univerſelle.*

The laſt two verſes were added when the hymn was appropriated to Paſſion-tide. The ending of Fortunatus is this:

"With fragrance dropping from each bough,
Sweeter than ſweeteſt nectar thou:
Decked with the fruit of peace and praiſe,
And glorious with Triumphal lays:—

"Hail, Altar! Hail, O Victim! Thee
Decks now Thy Paſſion's Victory;
Where Life for ſinners death endured,
And life by death for man procured."

VEXILLA REGIS.

FORTUNATUS.

I.

VEXILLA regis prodeunt,
Fulget crucis myſterium,
Quo carne carnis conditor
Suſpenſus eſt patibulo.

II.

Quo vulneratus inſuper
Mucrone diro lanceæ,
Ut nos lavaret crimine
Manavit unda ſanguine.

III.

Impleta ſunt quæ concinit
David fideli carmine
Dicens: In nationibus
Regnavit a ligno Deus.

THE VEXILLA REGIS.

DR. NEALE.

I.

THE Royal Banners forward go;
The Crofs fhines forth in myftic glow;
Where He in flefh, our flefh who made,
Our fentence bore, our ranfom paid.

2.

Where deep for us the fpear was dy'd,
Life's torrent rufhing from His fide,
To wafh us in that precious flood
Where mingled water flow'd, and blood.

3.

Fulfill'd is all that David told
In true prophetic fong of old;
Amidft the nations GOD, faith he,
Hath reign'd and triumph'd from the Tree.

IV.

Arbor decora et fulgida,
Ornata regis purpura,
Electa digno ſtipite
Tam ſancta membra tangere.

V.

Beata cujus brachiis
Pretium pependit ſæculi,
Statera facta ſæculi
Prædamque tulit tartaris.

VI.

O crux ave, ſpes unica!
Hoc paſſionis tempore,
Auge piis inſtitiam
Reiſque dona veniam.

VII.

Te ſumma Deus Trinitas
Collaudet omnis ſpiritus
Quas per crucis myſterium
Salvas, rege per ſæcula.

4.

O Tree of Beauty! Tree of Light!
O Tree with royal purple dight!
Elect on whose triumphal breast
Those holy limbs should find their rest!

5.

On whose dear arms, so widely flung,
The weight of this world's ransom hung:
The price of human kind to pay,
And spoil the Spoiler of his prey.

6.

O Cross, our one reliance, hail!
This holy Passion-tide, avail
To give fresh merit to the saint,
And pardon to the penitent.

7.

To Thee, Eternal Three in One,
Let homage meet by all be done;
Whom by the Cross Thou dost restore,
Preserve and govern evermore.

THE ALLELUIATIC SEQUENCE.

THIS famous Sequence, which may be regarded as the parent of every Hallelujah Chorus that has been written ſince, was composed by Godeſcalcus, prior to the year 950—the year of his death. The little that is known of him is given by his tranſlator.

"There is only one thing," ſays Dr. Neale, "with reſpect to the uſe of any of my hymns that has grieved me—the rejection of the noble melody of the ALLELUIATIC SEQUENCE, and that for a third-rate chant. What would be ſaid of chanting the *Dies Iræ?* And yet I really believe that it would ſuffer leſs than does the CANTEMUS CUNCTI by ſuch a ſubſtitution. Further, be it noticed, every ſentence—I had almoſt ſaid every word—of the verſion was carefully fitted to the muſic, and the length of the lines correſponds to the length of each *troparion* in the original."

"If it be ſaid that the original melody is difficult, I can only reply that I have frequently heard it ſung by a choir of children, of ages varying from four to fourteen; and never more prettily than when, without any accompaniment at all, in the open fields—the very ſmall ones joining in for the greater part with the whole of their little energy."—*Mediæval Hymns.*

CANTEMUS CUNCTI.

GODESCALCUS.

CANTEMUS cuncti melodum nunc
ALLELUIA.

II. In laudibus æterni regis hæc plebs resultet ALLELUIA.

III. Hoc denique cœlestes chori cantent in altum ALLELUIA.

IV. Hoc beatorum per prata paradisiaca psallat concentus ALLELUIA.

V. Quin et astrorum micantia luminaria jubilent altum ALLELUIA.

VI. Nubium cursus, ventorum volatus, fulgurum coruscatio et tonitruum sonitus dulce consonent simul
ALLELUIA.

THE ALLELUIATIC SEQUENCE.

DR. NEALE.

THE ſtrain upraiſe of joy and praiſe, *Alleluia.*
2. To the glory of their King
Shall the ranſom'd people ſing *Alleluia.*

3. And the Choirs that dwell on high
Shall re-echo through the ſky *Alleluia.*

4. They through the fields of Paradiſe that roam,
The bleſſed ones, repeat through that bright home *Alleluia.*

5. The planets glitt'ring on their heavenly way,
The ſhining conſtellations, join, and ſay *Alleluia.*

6. Ye clouds that onward ſweep!
Ye winds on pinions light!
Ye thunders, echoing loud and deep!
Ye lightnings, wildly bright!
In ſweet conſent unite your *Alleluia.*

VII. Fluctus et undæ, imber et procellæ, tempestas et serenitas, cauma, gelu, nix, prunæ, saltus, nemora pangant ALLELUIA.

VIII. Hinc variæ volucres creatorem laudibus concinite cum ALLELUIA.

IX. Ast illic respondeant voces altæ diversarum bestiarum ALLELUIA.

X. Istinc montium celsi vertices sonent ALLELUIA.

XI. Hinc vallium profunditates saltent ALLELUIA.

XII. Tu quoque maris jubilans abysse dic ALLELUIA.

XIII. Nec non terrarum molis immensitates: ALLELUIA.

XIV. Nunc omne genus humanum laudans exultet: ALLELUIA.

XV. Et creatori grates frequentans consonet: ALLELUIA.

XVI. Hoc denique nomen audire jugiter delectatur · ALLELUIA.

7. Ye floods and ocean billows!
Ye ſtorms and winter ſnow!
Ye days of cloudleſs beauty!
Hoar froſt and ſummer glow!
Ye groves that wave in ſpring,
And glorious foreſts, ſing *Alleluia.*

8. Firſt let the birds, with painted plumage gay,
Exalt their great CREATOR's praiſe, and ſay
Alleluia.

9. Then let the beaſts of earth, with varying ſtrain,
Join in Creation's Hymn, and cry again
Alleluia.

10. Here let the mountains thunder forth, ſonorous, *Alleluia.*

11. There, let the valleys ſing in gentler chorus,
Alleluia.

12. Thou jubilant abyſs of ocean, cry *Alleluia.*

13. Ye tracts of earth and continents, reply
Alleluia.

14. To GOD, who all Creation made,

15. The frequent hymn be duly paid: *Alleluia.*

16. This is the ſtrain, the eternal ſtrain, the LORD of all things loves: *Alleluia.*

XVII. Hoc etiam carmen cœleſte comprobat ipſe Chriſtus: ALLELUIA.

XVIII. Nunc vos ſocii cantate lætantes: ALLELUIA.

XIX. Et vos pueruli reſpondete ſemper ALLELUIA.

XX. Nunc omnes canite ſimul Alleluia domino, Alleluia Chriſto pneumatique ALLELUIA.

XXI. Laus Trinitati æternæ in babtiſmo domini quæ clarificatur: Hinc canamus: ALLELUIA.

17. This is the ſong, the heav'nly ſong, that
CHRIST Himſelf approves: *Alleluia.*
18. Wherefore we ſing, both heart and voice
awaking, *Alleluia.*
19. And children's voices echo, anſwer making,
Alleluia.
20. Now from all men be out-pour'd
Alleluia to the LORD;
With Alleluia evermore
The SON and SPIRIT we adore.
21. Praiſe be done to the THREE in ONE.
Alleluia! Alleluia! Alleluia! Alleluia!

APPENDIX.

THE concluding lines of the extract given at page 4, are in the original:

"Si tua nuncia prævenit uncia, surge, sequaris;
Expete limina, nulla gravamina jam verearis.
Si datur uncia, stat prope gratia Pontificalis;
Sin procul hæc valet, hæc tibi lex manet est schola talis."

The ninth and tenth stanzas of the STABAT MATER are more literally rendered in the following than in the version of Lord Lindsay. They also show the inability of the English double rhyme to express the pathos which invests the Latin.

"Let me with His stripes be rended;
Let me by His blood be cleansèd—
Looking to the Crucified.
Then, O Virgin, by thee lighted,
Wakened, warmed, aroused, excited,
For the judgment sanctified.

"Let me by the Cross directed,
By the death of CHRIST protected,
See below His glory far.
Then, this body mouldering, riven—
Then be to my spirit given
Paradisi Gloria!"

www.ingramcontent.com/pod-product-compliance
Lightning Source LLC
LaVergne TN
LVHW021414110826
845150LV00007B/1928

* 9 7 8 1 4 2 5 5 1 0 8 2 4 *